INTRODUCTION TO
POLITICS &
GOVERNMENTS

Janet Cook and Stephen Kirby
Edited by Judy Tatchell and Cheryl Evans
Designed by Chris Scollen

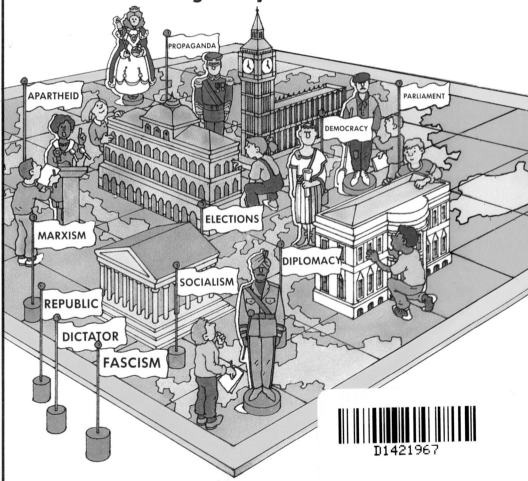

PROPAGANDA

APARTHEID

PARLIAMENT

DEMOCRACY

ELECTIONS

MARXISM

DIPLOMACY

SOCIALISM

REPUBLIC

DICTATOR

FASCISM

D1421967

Illustrated by Paddy Mounter, Adam Willis, Sue Walliker, Guy Smith, Sue Stitt, Chris Lyon and Brenda Haw

Editorial consultants: Dr Geoff Berridge (Department of Politics, Leicester University), Dr Patrick Considine (Lecturer in Comparative Philology, University College London) and Dr John Greenwood (School of Applied Social Sciences and Public Administration, Leicester Polytechnic).

Contents

First published in 1986 by Usborne Publishing Ltd. This edition published in 1990 by Usborne Publishing Ltd, Usborne House, 83-85 Saffron Hill, London EC1N 8RT, England.
Copyright © 1986 Usborne Publishing Ltd.

About this book

Every day, throughout the world, there are news stories in the papers or on the radio and television about politics. These stories are usually full of political jargon and ideas which can be confusing. This book explains the meanings, uses and origins of hundreds of the most common political terms.

Looking at ideologies

The first part of the book looks at the development of various political ideologies and beliefs. These include nationalism, liberalism, conservatism, communism, socialism and fascism. It explains what they mean and examines the words and ideas associated with them. There is also a look at the influential figures such as Plato and Marx.

Winning and exercising political power

A ballot paper and ballot box

The second part shows how political power can be won, for instance by a coup d'état or an election, and examines the differences between democracy and autocracy. There is also a look at the sets of laws, called constitutions, which lay down the way countries should be governed.

Political systems

The third part describes how various political systems work, with examples of a parliamentary system, a presidential system and a one-party system.

United Nations flag

International politics

Finally, the book goes into the world of international politics. There is a look at diplomacy and spying and also at alternative ways of putting pressure on another government, such as economic sanctions and force.

On pages 42-43 you can find out about various international organizations and alliances. These include the United Nations, the European Community, the Commonwealth of Nations, the Arab League, the Organization of African Unity, the North Atlantic Treaty Organization and the Warsaw Pact.

Pages 44-45 look at political parties in various countries and what they stand for. You can find out the names of the main political institutions in these countries, and the titles of their political leaders.

The aims of the book

The writers of this book have attempted, in explaining political words, ideas and systems, to be as unbiased as possible. This has not been easy, since political words often become slogans (or insults) and can change their meaning or mean different things to different people. There are therefore bound to be some explanations and definitions in this book with which some people may disagree.

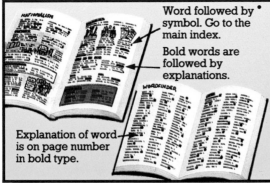

Word followed by • symbol. Go to the main index.

Bold words are followed by explanations.

Explanation of word is on page number in bold type.

How to use this book

On each page, the words printed in bold type are accompanied by definitions or explanations. Word boxes on every double page describe the origins of some of these words.

Words followed by a • symbol are defined elsewhere. To find the definition, refer to the Index on pages 46-48. The number of the page where the word is defined is printed in bold type.

3

What is politics?

There are always likely to be differing opinions and interests amongst a group of people. For example, a family may disagree over who should do certain chores such as the cooking or washing up. On a larger scale, members of a country may think differently about issues that affect them all. The Greek philosopher, **Aristotle** (384-322 BC), said that **politics** was the art of controlling these differing interests within a state and reaching an agreement on them. A **state** is a community which has its own government. Someone actively involved in politics is a **politician**.

What is an ideology?

Throughout history, people have invented theories about how a state should be run and what the order of priorities should be when decisions are made on political issues. These theories are called **ideologies**. You can find out about some of the main ideologies on the next few pages.

The first book about politics was the **Republic** written by **Plato** in the fourth century BC.* Aristotle studied under Plato.

REPUBLIC ~ BY ~ PLATO

Left-wing and right-wing

Aristocrats on the King's right.

Non-aristocrats on the King's left.

The King was imprisoned in October 1789.

These terms were first used in a political sense during the French Revolution. In 1789, King Louis XVI was forced to hold meetings with members of the clergy, nobility and middle classes (together known as the Estates General). At these meetings, the nobility sat on the King's right, and the others sat on his left. After the overthrow of the King, this custom spread to the French Assemblies. Those representing the aristocrats and tradition sat on the right, and those believing in more social equality* sat on the left.

Today, the socialist* ideology is said to be left-wing, and the conservative* ideology is said to be right-wing.

Political parties

A political **party** is a group which holds, or aims to hold, political power by becoming the government. The **government** is the group responsible for making political decisions and carrying out **policies**, or courses of action. A party's approach to politics may be based on an ideology but may be flexible when confronting the problems of the day. When a party tries to introduce fundamental changes in a political system, it is said to be **radical**. In some countries, many political parties compete to become the government. In others, such as China, only one party exists.

4

The exact date when Plato finished writing it is not known.
***See page 6 for more about the French Revolution.*

Types of government

There are two main types of government: democratic governments and autocratic governments.* Democratic governments depend on the support of their people to stay in power. Autocratic governments initiate and carry out policies with less respect for public opinion.

Below are some political problems facing a government and the different attitudes it might have towards them.

Here are some different attitudes to four political problems.

National defence

A country should make sure it is armed to such an extent that no other country would dare attack it.

Unemployment

It is the state's responsibility to provide enough jobs for everyone.

Enormous sums of money spent on national defence would be better spent on services such as health care or education.

It is each person's responsibility to find and compete for jobs. This ensures that each job vacancy is filled by the best person for it.

Businesses and people earning high incomes should pay heavy taxes in order to support those with less money.

Providing excellent social services discourages people from working hard and looking after themselves.

Taxation

High taxation reduces people's urge to work hard and earn more.

It is the state's responsibility to care for the poor and underprivileged by providing excellent social services such as hospitals and good housing for everyone.

Social services

Word box

Politics comes from the Greek word *polis,* meaning city state.

State comes from the Latin word *status,* meaning condition or circumstances.

Ideology comes from the Greek words *idea* meaning an ideal, and *logos* meaning explanation or argument.

Party comes from the Latin word *partire,* to divide. People divide up into political groups, or parties, according to their views on political issues and ideologies.

Government is based on the Latin word *gubernare,* to steer. A government is responsible for directing a country.

Policy comes from the Greek word *politeia,* meaning government of the *polis* (city-state).

Radical comes from the late Latin *radicalis,* from *radix,* meaning root.

5

*You can find out more about democratic and autocratic governments on pages 14-17.

Nationalism

For centuries the world has been divided up into different countries or states°. The sense of loyalty to a country is called **patriotism**. **Nationalism** is similar to patriotism but includes ideas about who should govern a country and how.

The **nationalist** ideology° first emerged during the **French Revolution**.

The French Revolution

Before the French Revolution, France was a **monarchy** (a country that is ruled, or whose government° is headed, by a King or Queen). The belief was that the monarch's powers were granted by God. This was called the **Divine Right of Kings**. Towards the end of the 18th century, this belief was being challenged. In June 1789, the French people were granted the right to form a **National Assembly** to advise King Louis XVI and restrict his power.

The Bastille in Paris was a state prison symbolizing the power of the monarchy.

Liberté, égalité, fraternité!

This was the revolutionaries' **slogan**, or catch-phrase. It means "freedom, equality and brotherhood".

The first nationalists wanted France to be a **republic** (a state° governed by representatives° of the people, without a King or Queen). They argued that a **nation** (see below) should have a government chosen from and by its people. This was the birth of the nationalist ideology.

The **Bastille** was stormed on 14 July 1789. In April 1792, Austria and Prussia (northern Germany) threatened to invade France to protect Louis XVI and the monarchical system. France declared war on Austria. Attitudes hardened against the King who was executed on 21 January 1793.

After the Revolution

To the revolutionaries, nationalism meant being able to elect their own government°. The ideology° of liberalism (freedom of the individual) also emerged.* The defenders of traditional political beliefs became known as conservatives.*

What is a nation?

Soon after the Revolution, different ideas began to emerge about what made up a nation. You can see some of these ideas below.

The Germans believed that nations were defined by language and culture. A person brought up in the German tradition would have German characteristics.

A French philosopher called Ernest Renan said that as well as common characteristics, people within a nation should feel united. Thus a nation might have a history in which the people took pride.

America used to be a British colony (governed by Britain). It declared itself to be independent on 4 July 1776. This meant that it could form its own government°.

For example, people from all over the world have emigrated to the USA and they speak many languages. Yet most take pride in the American War of Independence.**

*There is more about liberalism and conservatism on pages 8-9.
**More about the American War of Independence on page 32.

Patriotism

Nationalism is often confused with patriotism, which existed long before the French Revolution. Below you can see some examples of patriotism.

1. Many people respond to their national flag and anthem and are pleased when their country does well in the World Cup or the Olympics. When people go abroad, they often compare their country to the one they are travelling in.

2. Patriotism and nationalism prevent countries in the European Community* from acting as one unit. Member states still see themselves as separate and their interests often clash with those of the Community as a whole.

3. Patriotic feeling in the United Kingdom in 1982 ran high during the conflict with Argentina over the Falklands. This could be seen in newspaper headlines. People gave a lot of money to collections for the war effort.

Pros and cons of nationalism

Nationalism can be a good thing or a bad thing. Below you can find out some pros and cons of nationalism.

Pros

1. Nationalism can give people a pride in and a sense of belonging to a nation. This can make them take a constructive interest in the affairs of their country and respect its institutions and laws.

2. It can make a group more independent. Nationalist demands played a large part in persuading Britain, France, Holland and Portugal to grant independence to their colonies. A **colony** is a country governed by another country. After they are granted **independence**, they govern themselves.

Cons

1. It can cause a state* to become aggressive. For example, Hitler demanded that all German speaking people (such as those in Austria, Czechoslovakia and Poland) should join the German **Reich**, or German State. These foreign policies* led to the Second World War.

2. It can lead to instability where people in one country identify with more than one nation. For example, the Protestant "loyalist" majority in Northern Ireland identifies with Britain and wishes to remain within the United Kingdom. Many of the Catholic minority, however, identify with the Irish nation and wish to join the Irish Republic.

Word box

Nationalism and **nation** come from the Latin *natio* meaning birth, species or race.
Monarchy comes from the Greek word *monarchia* meaning rule by one person.
Republic comes from the Latin *res publica*, the state*. This is based on *res* (affair) and *publica* (public).
Bastille comes from the Old French word *bastir*, to build.

Slogan comes from the Gaelic words *sluagh* (army) and *gairm* (shout). This was because it originally referred to a war-cry.
Reich comes from the Old High German word *richi*, meaning kingdom, which comes from the Celtic *rix*, meaning king.
Colony comes from the Latin word *colonia*, meaning a farm or settlement.

*More about the European Community on page 45.

Liberalism and conservatism

The ideologies* of **liberalism** and **conservatism** first emerged during the French Revolution at the end of the 18th century (see page 6). Some revolutionaries were fighting for individual rights* and freedoms. They were **liberals**. After the Revolution, those who disagreed with them began to call themselves **conservatives**. They wanted to conserve, or keep, the old order.

18th century liberalism

18th century liberals believed that a government* should interfere with the lives of ordinary people as little as possible. This contrasted with the power exercised by the monarchs*. They put forward two ways to do this.

1. There should be laws setting out people's rights* and freedoms, such as those below.

Freedom of speech*.

Freedom of the press.

The right of everyone to take part in choosing a government.

Freedom to hold meetings.

The right to trade freely without government control.

2. A government's role should be limited. It should only be allowed to do what is absolutely necessary to protect people's lives and property and to defend their country against foreign attack.

How liberalism developed

Here you can see how the liberal ideology* developed in England, France, Germany and the USA towards the end of the 19th century.

In England, liberals believed that the government* should step in to free people from poverty and misery. This caused problems as they seemed to be saying contradictory things. On the one hand, they wanted to limit the powers of the government. On the other hand, they wanted to increase them to help the poor and uneducated.

The British **welfare state**, where the government provides such things as schooling, health care and old age pensions, began to develop in the late 19th century.

In Germany, two groups emerged. The first believed in limited government, like early liberals. The second was nationalistic.* It wanted to create a powerful German state• to protect the rights of the German people in world affairs. The German people would find freedom from belonging to and supporting this perfect state.

The interpretations of liberalism that developed in England also developed in France. The group that wanted a strong government to promote freedom from poverty and so on said that such a government would not interfere with liberty so long as it was supported by most of the people.

When he was young, Napoleon Bonaparte was a liberal. Later he became a very conservative **emperor**.

Although liberalism in the USA mostly meant freedom from poverty, the principle of freedom from government was strongly upheld in the American constitution.**

Conservatism

Conservatism argues that traditions and customs that have grown up in a society survive because they work. The established way of doing things is likely to be better than the new and untried.

Comparing conservatism with liberalism

Unlike conservatism, liberalism regards tradition as a barrier to progress.

Like early liberalism, conservatism says that the role of the government• should be limited to defending a country and keeping law and order. However conservatism puts less emphasis than liberalism upon the government being responsible for welfare. People should be as independent as possible. Unlike liberalism, conservatism is often said to be **reactionary**, that is, it expresses the wish to go back to the political systems of the past.

The pieces on the board below show you some of the things that conservatism supports.

The right to acquire, keep and inherit wealth.

The Church

The home and family

Royal families

Conservatism accepts that some degree of social and political inequality is both beneficial and inevitable.

Word box

Liberal comes from the Latin *liber,* meaning free.
Conservative comes from the Latin *conservare* meaning to maintain or keep safe.
Welfare state is based on the English word welfare (fare-well in reverse), which means getting on well.
Emperor comes from the Latin *imperator* (commander).
Reactionary comes from the French *réaction,* reversing or undoing. This is based on the Latin *re-,* again or against, and *actio,* doing or acting (from *agere,* to do or act).

9

*See pages 6-7 for more about nationalism.
**There is more about the American constitution on pages 32-33.

Communism

Communism in early societies, such as in some medieval monasteries, meant that all property belonged jointly to everyone in the group or community. More recently, the flower power communes in California during the 1960s and 1970s also worked like this. People shared clothes, food and so on.

Communism as an ideology*,

however, is mainly based on the ideas of **Karl Marx** (1818-1883) who was a German Jew. In his book, **_The Communist Manifesto_**, he predicted the end of the existing system, called capitalism. You can find out more about this below. You can also see how his ideas were developed by other major political leaders such as Lenin and Mao.

What is capitalism?

The word **capital** means all the money, property and equipment used for carrying on a business. Sometimes people use it to mean their property and money they have saved in a bank.

Capitalism is a system where the means of production (industries, businesses and so on) are owned by a relatively small group. These people, called shareholders, invest money in companies by buying shares. In return they get a share of the profits.

Marx's arguments against capitalism

Hard work by the = Money in the pockets
proletariat   of the bourgeoisie.

Marx was deeply concerned about the poverty of the workers, whom he called the **proletariat**. He believed that the group in control (the **bourgeoisie**) took advantage of them and paid them low **wages**. Most of the rewards for their work went to the bourgeoisie in the form of profits.

Marx's solution

Marx's theories are known as **Marxism**. He believed that the proletariat would rebel against capitalism and communism would take its place. This would happen in two stages:

"Let the governing classes tremble before the communist revolution. The proletarians have nothing to lose in it but their chains. They have the whole world to gain. Working men of all countries, unite!"

Stage 1. There would be a **dictatorship of the masses** with the proletariat having power over the bourgeoisie. Everything would be taken into state* ownership. He called this the **socialist stage**.

Stage 2.

To the state: Results and profits from hard work.

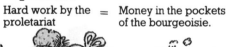

From the state:
Food
Money
Clothes
Housing

From each according to his abilities, to each according to his needs.

Conflict between the bourgeoisie and the proletariat would end. All goods and services would be shared out on the basis of each person's needs. In return, everyone would work as hard as possible.

Adapting Marxism

1. V. I. Ulyanov Lenin (1870-1924)

Lenin led the **Russian revolution** in 1917. Until recently, his theories were the basis of Russian and international communism.

By the beginning of the 20th century, Marx's predicted revolution[*] had still not taken place. In 1902, a Russian called **Lenin** published a pamphlet called *What is to be done?* in which he made some amendments to Marxism. He said that his amendments adapted Marxism to the 20th century.

Lenin's main comment was that the proletariat would not be able to organize a revolution on their own. A **vanguard** (an advance group) who would act in their name would need to start it. The vanguard and proletariat would form a party[*] to work in the interests of the proletariat. They must be united and there should be no opposition to the party.

2. Mao Zedong (Mao Tse Tung)[*] (1893-1976)

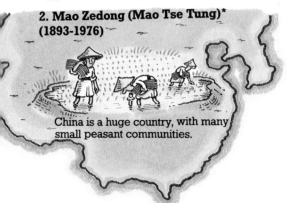

China is a huge country, with many small peasant communities.

Mao Zedong adapted Marxism to the agricultural society of China. He believed that **manual labour** (working with the hands) was superior to any other form of labour and that peasants were to be respected above any other group. Unlike Lenin, he declared that opposition to the communist party should be allowed. If there was an argument between the party and the peasants, the peasants should win. However, critics of communism under Mao say that in practice he did not allow opposition to the party.

3. Eurocommunism

Eurocommunists wish to adapt the communist ideals to the needs of their own countries, without resorting to revolution[*].

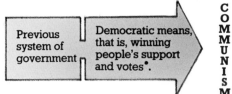

Previous system of government → Democratic means, that is, winning people's support and votes[*]. → COMMUNISM

The French and Italian communist parties drew up the *Eurocommunist Manifesto* in 1975. In it, they declared themselves to be anti-revolution and argued against Marx's first stage (dictatorship of the masses).

The decline of communism

Economic failure and general discontent steadily undermined communism. Gorbachev, who came to power in Russia in 1985, began a reform to revitalise the Soviet system and communism generally. This led to the freeing of Eastern Europe from communist oppression and has opened the way for the USSR to become a democratic[*] society.

Word box

Communism comes from the Latin *communis*. This word was based on *com*, meaning together, and *munus*, meaning duty or service.

Capitalism comes from the Latin *caput*, meaning head. This is because capital is a chief or principal sum of money.

Proletariat comes from the Latin *proletarius*. This was a citizen[*] of Ancient Rome of the sixth and lowest class, who served the state[*] not with his property but with his *proles*, or offspring. These would provide more workers.

Bourgeoisie comes from the French *bourgeois*, a citizen.

Wage comes from the Middle English *wage*. This in turn derives from the Germanic word *wadjan*, meaning pledge or promise. The employer promised to pay the worker for his labour.

Vanguard is a military term meaning the part of the army that goes in front. The word comes from the French *avant-garde* (*avant* means before, and *garde* means a guard).

Manual comes from the Latin *manus*, meaning hand.

11

*In 1949 the Chinese updated their spelling of certain names and places. Mao Zedong is the new spelling.

Socialism

Like communism•, **socialism** makes equality of income and wealth a high priority. It argues that it is a government's• responsibility to work towards this. Many people see socialism as an end in itself, though Marx• saw it as a temporary stage between capitalism• and full communism.* Below are some examples of socialist goals.

Social justice: The government should make sure that everyone has good health care, education and housing.

Egalitarianism or **equality:** Everyone should have equal rights•. The government ought to ensure a fair distribution of wealth.

Public ownership: Socialists argue that capitalism produces inequalities. Major industries should therefore be **nationalized** (owned by the state•).

Origins of socialism

1. Some aspects of socialism go back as far as the fourth century BC when Plato• wrote the *Republic•*. He suggested that rulers should hold their possessions in common.

2. In 1516, **Thomas More** wrote a book called *Utopia*. In it he described an ideal society made up of groups of people working together and sharing the profits equally.

3. Although most French revolutionaries** were fighting for political rights•, some claimed that communally owned property was also a basic right.

Active socialism

Some socialists believe in fast change and strong action, such as mass strikes, to achieve their goals. They are called **activists**. Before the late 19th century, socialism was mainly an activist ideology•. A current example of an activist group is **Militant** in Britain.

Social democracy

In the 1870s a section of the socialist movement broke away from the traditional activist outlook of the movement. They believed in slow change achieved through existing political systems. In 1884 the **Fabian Society** was formed in Britain. It favoured improving social conditions by reform whenever the opportunity arose.

Word box

Socialism comes from the Latin *socius*, meaning a companion.
Egalitarianism and **equality** come from the Latin *aequalis*, meaning equal.
Utopia comes from the Greek *ou*, meaning not, and *topos*, a place. It is an idealized place that does not exist.

Militant is from the Latin *militare*, to serve as a soldier. It refers to people who are prepared to fight for their aims.
Fabian comes from the Roman General, Quintus Fabius Maximus. He believed that success would come through a gradual wearing down of the enemy.

*See pages 10-11 for more about Marx and communism.
**See pages 6-7 for more about the French Revolution.

Fascism

Fascism is an ideology* which was first developed by **Benito Mussolini** after he seized power in Italy in 1922. However, the term is sometimes applied to the ideas of other **dictators** (rulers whose words are law) such as **Hitler** in Germany, **Franco** in Spain and **Peron** in Argentina.

What is fascism?

Unlike most other ideologies*, fascism is not based on a distinct set of beliefs. Instead, it describes certain attitudes and types of behaviour. Below are some characteristics of the fascist states* of Mussolini's Italy and Hitler's Germany.

1. Both Mussolini and Hitler were hostile to philosophy, reason and rights*. Their policies* were largely based on instinct. Mussolini said that he could smell what was the right action to take.

2. Mussolini and Hitler claimed absolute obedience from the people. They attracted great admiration and support.

3. Italy and Germany were **totalitarian** states. This means that the state allows no rival political parties* and controls every aspect of the lives of its citizens. Duty to the state is more important than any other tie, such as the Church or family.

These are medals that Mussolini gave his soldiers for bravery.

4. Mussolini believed that action was superior to thought. He said that just as fighting set a seal of nobility on the individual, war* set a seal of nobility on the nation*.

5. Fascists in Hitler's Germany were also racist. **Racism** is the belief that one race is superior to another. Hitler believed that "true" German people (whom he called **Aryans**) were a superior race who were destined to rule the world.

6. German fascists were especially hostile to Jews. This attitude is called **anti-semitism**. Hitler believed that Germany's past failures were the result of an international conspiracy against Germany organized by the Jews.

Word box

Fascism comes from the Latin *fasces*. This describes the bundle of wooden rods with an axe in the middle which was carried before high officials in Ancient Rome. The bundle signified social unity, and the axe, the authority of the political leadership. Nowadays, the word "fascist" is often mistakenly used as a term of abuse for anyone with extreme right-wing* views.

Dictator comes from the Latin *dictare*, to declare, order or dictate.
Totalitarian comes from the Latin *totus* meaning whole.
Aryan comes from the Sanskrit word *aryas*, meaning noble.
Semitism comes from *Sem*, the Greek form of the Hebrew name *Shem*. A Semite is a person who is said to be descended from Shem, one of the sons of Noah.

Democracy

There are two main forms of government°, **democracy** and autocracy°. On these two pages you can find out what a democracy is and about different types of democracy. (You can find out about autocracy on pages 16-17.)

The idea of democracy originated in Ancient Greece. It means rule by the people.

> A **citizen** is a member of a state° or country who has certain political rights°, such as the right to vote.

> In Ancient Athens, women and slaves were not regarded as citizens.

Direct democracy

In certain Ancient Greek cities, such as Athens, citizens would meet in the market place to discuss problems which affected them all. People made speeches to try to get support for their views. The citizens then voted° and the view which gained the most votes would win. This way of making decisions, where each citizen is involved, is called **direct democracy**.

Direct democracy worked in Athens because there were less than 4,000 citizens. The size of modern states makes direct democracy impractical today except in certain circumstances where a **referendum** is held. This is when the government° asks all citizens to vote on a single important issue. For example, a referendum was held in Spain in 1986 to decide if the country should stay in NATO*.

Representative liberal democracy

In many countries today, decisions are made on the votes° of only a few hundred people who are elected (chosen) by the citizens.** They make decisions on behalf of all the citizens and are known as representatives°. They often belong to a political party°. All citizens have the right to vote and put themselves forward as possible representatives, called candidates°. This is known as **representative liberal democracy**.

Below you can find out some of the characteristics of a representative liberal democracy.

1. There must be more than one candidate to choose from.

2. Candidates may oppose the government° of the day.

3. Voters may vote for any candidate they choose, free from unfair pressure.

4. Elections° must be held every few years.

*NATO stands for North Atlantic Treaty Organisation. See page 42.
**You can find out more about elections and voting on pages 22-26.

Protecting minority groups

Representative liberal democracies have laws to protect the rights[•] of individuals and minorities such as racial or religious minorities. Without them, a situation could occur in which the majority ignores the interests and rights of these minorities. This is called "the tyranny of the majority". The laws designed to protect minorities are often contained in a country's constitution. You can find out more about constitutions on pages 18-19.

Democracy in communist states

Some communist[•] one-party states[•] used to call themselves democracies. They said their policies[•] were in the best interest of all, so there was no need for other parties[•]. But reformed communists now say that if there is no political choice, it is not a democracy. By the late 1980s, many communist parties started to move towards genuine democracy. Some have have been peacefully replaced. Others, such as the Communist Party of the Soviet Union (CPSU)* are shedding their communist character.

In Russia, the CPSU used to choose the candidates[•] who stood, unopposed, for election[•]. People simply confirmed this decision when they voted[•]. You can see how elections work in the West on pages 22-26.

How democratic are modern democracies?

Some people believe that Western democracies are not democratic enough. Here are some of the things they say:

Most political decisions have different effects on the rich and poor. People in Western democracies vote[•] for what is best for them.

Once elected, representatives use their own judgement when making decisions. This may not always coincide with public opinion.

Important decisions should be decided by referendums and not left entirely to the government.

People can be influenced by the **media** (newspapers, television and radio). Often the media reflects the views of powerful groups, or a particular political party or cause.

Word box

Democracy comes from the Greek word *demokratia* meaning people-rule. It is based on the words *demos,* the people, and *kratos,* power or authority.
Citizen comes from the Anglo-Norman word *citezein*. This is based on the Latin *civitas,* meaning city.
Referendum comes from the Latin *referre,* to carry back, report or refer for consideration.
Media comes from the Latin *medium,* meaning middle.

*See pages 34-35 for more about the CPSU.

Autocracy

Autocracy is opposite in meaning to democracy (see previous two pages). One person or group holds all the power. The power-holder may be an individual, a family, a political party* or a group of military officers. They do not allow opposition of any kind.

Here you can find out about different kinds of autocracy.

Royal dynasties

A **royal dynasty** is a royal family with total political power. The power is passed to a son or daughter when the ruler dies or **abdicates** (gives up power). There are a number of dynastic royal families in the Arab world. In Europe, however, most royal families have no real political power any more. Until the Russian Revolution* in 1917, Russia was ruled by a dynasty called the Romanovs. The ruler was called a **Tsar**.

Family dictatorships

A dictator* is someone whose word is law. A **family dictatorship** is an autocracy where power is held by a non-royal family that imposes its rule by force.

An example was the Duvalier family in Haiti in the Caribbean. François Duvalier (Papa Doc) was elected* President* in 1957. He quickly disposed of existing systems of government* and ruled as a dictator.

He had his own private army known as the **Tonton Macoute**. They intimidated people, for example by voodoo methods (see below), and tortured and killed political opponents. Although there was supposed to be an election every six years, Duvalier never allowed any. He created himself President for life in 1964. He died in 1971 and was succeeded by his son,

Jean-Claude Duvalier (Baby Doc), who stayed in power until 1986, when massive opposition forced him to abdicate.

Voodoo

Voodoo is a kind of magic based on superstition. Voodooists may wear frightening masks and use other scary props. To work, it depends on people believing it can harm them.

Individual dictatorships

Individual dictatorships are similar to family dictatorships, except that power does not pass on to the son or daughter. Again, power is imposed by force. One example was Nicolae Ceausescu who headed a terrorist regime in Romania until he was overthrown by a mass uprising in 1989. Other contemporary examples include Colonel Gadaffi in Libya and Saddam Hussein in Iraq.

*See page 34 for more about the Russian Revolution.
**See pages 22-23 for more about political parties.

Military dictatorships

This is when political power is held by a military council. It often imposes **martial law**, under which military law courts are set up and soldiers keep law and order. Laws and penalties are much stricter. The council may set up a **curfew**. This is a period, usually at night, when no one is allowed on the streets. A bell or other signal marks the start and end of the curfew. Curfews were first used in medieval France. They marked the time of evening when home fires had to be extinguished for safety.

Often there is a struggle for power. When one military leader overthrows another it is called a **putsch**.

One-party states

A **one-party state** is a state where only one party is allowed to exist. Examples are Hitler's Germany, Mussolini's Italy and communist states such as Albania and China. Citizens usually have few rights[•].

In Africa today, many countries which have recently gained independence[•] are one-party states. They argue that if there were several parties, different tribes would support different parties. Having just one party makes it easier to create a common national[•] identity.

One-religion states

An Islamic temple or mosque.

In **one-religion states**, all the political power is concentrated in a religious organization. Examples are Iran under Ayatollah Khomeini and Pakistan under General Zia. Both are Islamic states[•]. All senior positions in the state are held by Islamic politicians.

Benevolent autocracies

Most autocracies have a poor record of human rights* and are rarely supported by the majority of their citizens[•]. This is not always the case, however. Many Arab dynasties are **benevolent autocracies**. They provide a high standard of living and education.

Word box

Autocracy comes from the Greek *autos,* meaning self, and *kratos,* power.
Dynasty comes from the Greek *dynasthai,* meaning to be able, or to have power.
Abdicate is from the Latin *abdicare* meaning to refuse, renounce or resign.
Tsar (or Czar) comes from the Latin *Caesar,* a name given to Roman Emperors after Julius Caesar. The German *Kaiser,* meaning Emperor, also comes from this.
Tonton Macoute is Creole for Bogeyman.
Martial comes from the Latin *martialis,* belonging to Mars, the Roman god of war.
Curfew comes from the Anglo-Norman *coeverfu,* meaning to cover fire.
Putsch is a Swiss-German expression for a thrust or blow.
Benevolent comes from the Latin *benevolens,* meaning well-wishing.

*You can find out more about human rights on pages 18-19.

Constitutions

Most countries have a set of laws, separate from other laws of the land, which lay down the way the country should be governed. This is known as a **constitution**.

A constitution normally tells you three things. Firstly, it defines the role and powers of the main branches of government•. Secondly, it states whether there is more than one level of government. Finally, it lays out the rights of the citizens•.

Branches of government

The executive

The **executive** makes and carries out government• policy•. In the UK, it consists of the Prime Minister•, the Cabinet• and junior ministers•. In the USA it is made up of the President• and the heads of major departments of state such as the Treasury.

CONSTITUTION

The three rows of boxes on the right tell you about the three main areas that a constitution normally covers.

Levels of government

The constitution lays down how many levels of government• a country has. Each level usually has an executive, legislature and jucidiary. If there is more than one, it defines their relationship. A system may be unitary*, federal* or confederal.

Federal and confederal systems

The country is divided into states• or regions. It has two levels of government, the national and the state. The national government makes policies• that concern the whole country. State institutions make their own laws on internal affairs.

Unitary systems

Countries which do not have federal or confederal systems have unitary systems. One central government is responsible for the whole country. It may have several local government authorities, such as the French *départements,* to carry out services delegated by the central government.

Unwritten constitutions

Some countries such as the UK and Israel have "unwritten" constitutions. Instead of having a single document, their rules are contained partly in ordinary laws and partly in customs and conventions.

Sham constitutions

The contents of a constitution and what happens in practice vary considerably. Some autocratic• governments• can use a constitution to make them appear democratic•.

Citizens' rights

The constitution normally defines the **political** and **human rights** of citizens• which the government• should respect. In practice, these are often ignored.

The USA and West Germany are federal systems. Britain and France are unitary.

In the UK it is made up of the House of Commons* and the House of Lords*.

In the USA it is known as Congress* and consists of the House of Representatives* and the Senate*.

The legislature

The **legislature** examines executive policy and normally has to approve it before it can be carried out. It passes laws and raises funds, through taxation, that the policies require. In the picture above, you can see how the legislatures in the UK and the USA are made up.

The judiciary

These are the law courts responsible for interpreting the laws of the state* and judging those who break them. Some countries have a special court, such as the Supreme Court* in the USA, which decides if the actions of the executive and legislature fall within the powers given to them by the constitution.

The difference between federal and confederal systems

In a federal system, such as the USA, the laws of state* governments* can be questioned by national government. It can refer a state law to a special court in the judiciary if it thinks that the law is **unconstitutional**, that is, contrary to the spirit of the constitution.

In a confederal system, the states are more independent and have more individual responsibility. The Swiss Confederation has 22 Cantons. It is very rare for the central government to challenge the laws of the Cantons.

The minimum age required to obtain a driving licence varies between American states. In Mississippi, you have to be 15, whereas in Colorado you must be 16.

Political rights

These may include the right to vote*, **freedom of speech** (the right to criticize the state*), the right to oppose the government and the freedom to form groups such as Trade Unions*, which protect the rights of employees.

Human rights

These include the right to a fair trial and freedom from inhumane punishment and unjust arrest. Some constitutions have laws against **discrimination** (different treatment) on the basis of race, religion, or sex.

Word box

Constitution comes from the Latin *constitutio*, arrangement or order.
Executive comes from the Latin *exsequi*, to follow up, carry out or execute.
Legislature comes from the Latin *legislator*, which means law-giver.
Judiciary comes from the Latin *iudicum*, meaning court.
Unitary comes from the Latin *unus*, one.
Federal comes from the Latin *foedus*, meaning a league, alliance or treaty.
Confederal comes from the Latin *confoederare* meaning to join in a league.
Discrimination comes from the Latin *discriminare*, to separate.

Pressure groups

Pressure groups put pressure on the government* to try to influence decisions on issues they feel are important. These may be relevant only to the group or to society as a whole. A pressure group differs from a political party* in that it does not seek to become the government and usually has limited aims. It may be associated with a political party, though.

Putting on the pressure

Here are the four main areas where pressure groups apply pressure.

1. The government ministers* and their administrators (Civil Servants*) who are responsible for the group's area of interest.

When pressure groups meet politicians to try to gain their support, it is called lobbying.

2. Representatives* in the legislature*. Some pressure groups even sponsor a representative. For example, most members of the US Congress* are paid by groups to represent their interests.

3. The general public and the media*. For example, the anti-nuclear movement holds demonstrations to show the strength of public support. Some groups also produce publicity material, called **propaganda**, aimed at winning support.

4. The judiciary*. For example, the Civil Rights Movement in the USA won the vote for coloured Americans in the Supreme Court*. In Europe, human rights* issues can be taken to the European Court.

Pros and cons of pressure groups

Pros

1. They provide a way of protesting against unpopular policies* and force governments* to respond to public opinion between elections*.
2. Pressure groups with different views on an issue give the government an all-round picture.

Cons

1. Discussions between a pressure group and a politician or Civil Servant* are held in private. Decisions may therefore be made using information that is kept from the rest of the legislature*. This is undemocratic and may also be open to corruption.

2. Large or wealthy groups have more influence. For example, manufacturers have more power than consumer organizations. In some countries, the food industry prevents strict laws about food additives, though some people think they are harmful.

Some famous pressure groups

Anti-Apartheid Movement
They fight for the vote* and other human and political rights* for coloured people under the **apartheid** (separation of races) system in South Africa.

Financial institutions such as Wall Street (USA)
These have no organized pressure group, but exert influence on governments*.

Greenpeace
Members are concerned with environmental issues, such as their Save the Whale campaign*.

*More about political parties on pages 22-23.

How much power do pressure groups have?

The power of pressure groups can vary greatly. Here are some of the vital factors involved.

1. Number of members. A large group will usually have more impact on the government* and public at large than a small one.

2. Economic "muscle". For example, a Trade Union, such as a power workers' union, could close down all the power stations.

> A **Trade Union** is an association of employees. It protects their interests in such matters as wages* and working conditions.

3. Financial resources. These are for publicity material, postage, phone bills, wages for full-time workers and so on.

4. Public support. Some groups, such as nurses' unions, gain influence because they have the sympathy of the public.

5. Prestige. Many professional groups, such as lawyers or bankers, are powerful because society holds them in high esteem.

6. Information resources. For example, a government might need information from a farming union when deciding on subsidies.

Word box

Lobbying. This term arose because often the only part of a legislative building that is open to the public is the lobby. Members of pressure groups sometimes collect in the lobby in the hope of seeing a sympathetic representative*.

Propaganda comes from the Latin *propagare,* to propagate or extend. Nowadays it often has overtones of exaggeration or manipulation of facts.

Apartheid is an Afrikaans word meaning separateness. It is the policy* of dividing up the different races in South Africa and giving them unequal rights*.

International Cycling Union Based in Geneva, the group campaigns for better roads and conditions for cyclists all over the world.

Anti-nuclear movement These groups, such as CND* in Britain, believe that nuclear weapons should be banned worldwide.

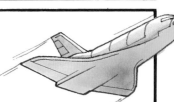

Trekkies The fan club of the American TV series *Star Trek* persuaded President Ford to change the name of the first Space Shuttle from *Constitution* to *Enterprise***.

*Campaign for Nuclear Disarmament.

**Enterprise is the name of the Star Trek spaceship.

Elections and political parties

An **election** is the choice of a political leader or representative° by a system of voting. **Voting** is how people express a preference. It may be done by a show of hands or by putting a mark beside a name on a piece of paper.

A **general election** is when all the voters in a country can vote. In many countries there are only general elections for the legislature°. The leader of the executive° is chosen by another method, such as by an election within the winning party°.

Winning an election

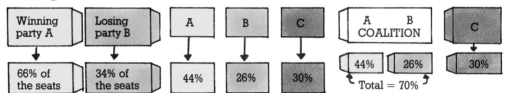

| Winning party A | Losing party B | | A | B | C | | A   B COALITION | | C |
| 66% of the seats | 34% of the seats | | 44% | 26% | 30% | | 44% | 26% | 30% |

Total = 70%

In elections for the legislature°, if a party's° **candidates** (proposed representatives°) win over half the places, or **seats**, the party is said to have a **clear majority**. In some countries, such as the UK and Australia, the majority party forms the executive°.

Where there are more than two parties competing, the winning party's majority may be less than the total of the other parties' seats. In Britain, this situation is called a **Hung Parliament**. The winning party could be outvoted in the legislature by the other parties.

A way round this situation is for the winning party to join with another party so that between them they have more than half the seats. This is called a **coalition**. Two weaker parties may form a coalition before an election to increase their joint chances of winning.

Why have elections?

1. Voters can take part in choosing political representatives° and leaders.
2. Elections are usually held every few years. Leaders therefore regularly have to justify their policies° if they want to be re-elected.

3. They allow a smooth change of political power from one party° to another.*
4. In autocratic° systems, they link the government° and its policies to the people, though the government may try to ignore the result.

Winning the vote

Many groups of people had to fight to be given the right to vote.

In the early 20th century, Emmeline Pankhurst formed a group of women known as **Suffragettes**. They fought for the vote for women in the United Kingdom.

In New Zealand, women were given the vote as early as 1893. In Switzerland, they did not get the vote until 1971.

In the USA, certain racial groups, such as the blacks in southern states, were denied the right to vote. Campaigns° on their behalf resulted in the Voting Rights Act of 1965. The fight for the vote for blacks, coloureds and Asians is still going on in South Africa.

Votes for women!

Suffragettes chained themselves to railings outside public buildings to try to gain public sympathy for their cause.

See pages 28-29 for some other methods of political change.

Who votes today?

Countries have different laws about who may vote. The major requirements are that you must be a citizen° of the country and have reached a certain age. The youngest age requirement is in the Philippines, where you have to be 15. The oldest is in Andorra where you have to be 25.

Rigged elections

In many countries, elections are often **rigged**, meaning that the true result is tampered with. In the 1986 presidential election in the Philippines, both candidates, the former President Marcos and his opponent, Cory Aquino, claimed to have won.

Another rigged election was the presidential election of 1927 in Liberia. President Charles King claimed a majority over his opponent of 234,000. The total number of voters was only 16,000.

The birth of political parties

Voting played a large part in Ancient Greek democracies*. After their decline, political decisions in most places tended to be made by an emperor°, monarch° or small group. Voting and elections were sometimes carried out within these privileged groups.

In the 19th century, the power of the rulers was challenged by newly rich manufacturers. The rulers were forced to include them by giving them the vote.

Soon industrial workers also demanded a say in politics°. Since they could bring industry to a halt if they refused to work, they had to be included.

Parties often adopt a colour or symbol. In America, the Republican party has an elephant as its symbol and the Democratic party has a donkey.**

As more people won the vote, politicians had to form organized political parties° to define what they stood for and to win support. They began to create political programmes and make election promises.

Mobilization and representative parties

There are two different types of political party°, called mobilization parties and representative parties.

Mobilization parties usually exist in one-party states°. The party consists of a relatively small group who make decisions and then claim they have popular support for them. For instance, the party may say it represents the interests of everyone, so it must have everyone's support.

Candidate from a representative party trying to win votes by making a speech.

A **representative party** responds to the views of its supporters and changes its policies° accordingly. It needs to do this because its popularity will be reflected in the number of seats it wins at the next election. Most parties in Western systems are representative.

Word box

Election comes from the Latin *electio*, meaning choosing or selection.
Vote comes from the Latin *votum*, a wish.
Candidate comes from the Latin *candidatus*. It is based on *candidus*, which means white. In Ancient Rome, candidates dressed in white.
Coalition comes from the Latin word *coalescere*, to unite or agree.
Suffragette is based on suffrage, meaning vote. It comes from the Latin *suffragium*, which means vote or the right to vote.

23

*See page 14 for more about democracy in Ancient Greece.
**See page 45 for more about the Republican and Democratic parties.

Campaigning for votes

Before an election*, parties* try to win votes* by running a **campaign**. This is a planned operation to persuade people to support them. Most countries have laws stating when campaigning can take place, such as a certain number of months before the election. Here are some of the ways parties campaign.

Parties hold meetings to explain and discuss their policies*. Anyone can attend and contribute.

Each party publishes a programme of policies that it promises to carry out if elected. This is called a **manifesto**.

They produce leaflets and posters for publicity.

Floating voters are people who do not support a particular party.

Television and radio campaigning

Parties* use television and radio to try to influence voters*. In some countries, parties or candidates* can buy air time. In others, such as the UK, all parties are given a share of radio and television time relating, for example, to the number of candidates put forward by each party.

Opinion polls

Opinion polls are an attempt to predict the outcome of an election* by questioning a group believed to be representative of the whole population.

Canvassing

Canvassing is making door-to-door calls to identify and win party* supporters.

You vote at a **polling station**.

POLLING STATION

They encourage supporters to vote* and may provide transport to the polling station.

This is called voting by **secret ballot**.

You mark your choice of candidate* on a **ballot paper** in private. It goes in the **ballot box**.

Word box

Campaign comes from the Latin *campus*, meaning field. It was first used to describe an army's operations in the field.
Manifesto is from the Latin *manifestare*, to make obvious or show plainly.
Poll is a Middle English word meaning head. A political poll is a head count of people's votes*.

Canvassing means tossing something in a canvas sheet. The political meaning may have arisen through the idea of shaking up or agitating opinions.
Ballot means a secret vote. It comes from the Italian *ballotta* meaning a little ball. In 16th century Venice people voted by placing small balls in a box.

Electoral systems

Most democratic° states° are divided into areas called **constituencies**. Each constituency has one or more **representatives** in the legislature°, depending on the system. Voters° choose who will represent them from a number of candidates°, most of whom have been put forward by a political party°.

On the next two pages you can find out about the four main ways in which elections° are held.

1. First past the post
This system is used in the UK. People vote° for the candidate° they wish to represent them. The candidate with the most votes wins.

A disadvantage of this system is that a party° might come second in many constituencies, getting a large number of votes° throughout the country. The number of seats° won by the party might not accurately reflect its popularity.

2. Second ballot

This system has recently been used in France.

Each constituency has one seat° in the legislature°. If a candidate° has a clear majority, that candidate wins.

A clear majority° is when someone gets more than 50% of the votes.

42%	29%	21%	8%

If there is no clear majority, the two candidates with the most votes° compete in a second election°. Everyone votes again for one of them.

The candidate who was runner-up in the first election may win the second by picking up votes previously cast for the weaker candidates.

48%	52%

3. Alternative vote

Voters° list the candidates° in order of preference. If no candidate has a clear majority on first preference, the one with the least votes is ruled out. This candidate's votes are then shared out on second preference, and so on until one candidate gets a clear majority.

Alternative vote ballot paper°

2	JON ARMSTRONG
3	JENNY GRANT
5	MICHAEL HILL
1	JOAN SMART
6	LUCY SMYTHE
4	PAT O'SULLIVAN

Word box
Constituency comes from the Latin *constituere*, to appoint. Members of a constituency (**constituents**) appoint a person to represent them in the legislature°.

Representative comes from the Latin *repraesentare*, to place before. A representative places the views of his or her constituents before the legislature.

Proportional representation (PR)

In this system each constituency* has a number of seats* in the legislature*. Like the Alternative Vote* system, voters* list candidates* in order of preference. There are many types of PR, the most common being the **Single Transferable Vote** shown in the example below. In the Killaloe constituency, there are five candidates competing for three seats.

Four candidates could get 150 votes but only three could get 151 or more. So you divide the votes cast by the seats available plus one (3 + 1) and add one to the answer.

There are 600 voters and three seats, so a candidate needs at least 151 votes to win a seat. This number is worked out as shown above. The chart below shows how votes are allocated and who wins the seats.

600 ÷ 4

Votes cast
Seats + 1

150

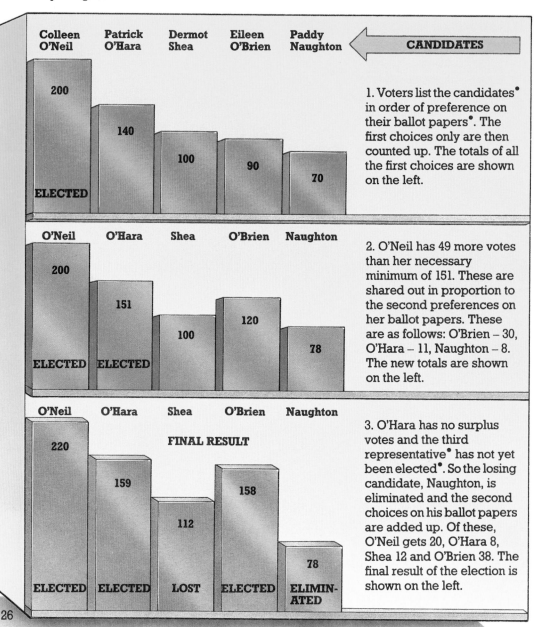

CANDIDATES

1. Voters list the candidates* in order of preference on their ballot papers*. The first choices only are then counted up. The totals of all the first choices are shown on the left.

Colleen O'Neil	Patrick O'Hara	Dermot Shea	Eileen O'Brien	Paddy Naughton
200	140	100	90	70
ELECTED				

2. O'Neil has 49 more votes than her necessary minimum of 151. These are shared out in proportion to the second preferences on her ballot papers. These are as follows: O'Brien – 30, O'Hara – 11, Naughton – 8. The new totals are shown on the left.

O'Neil	O'Hara	Shea	O'Brien	Naughton
200	151	100	120	78
ELECTED	ELECTED			

3. O'Hara has no surplus votes and the third representative* has not yet been elected*. So the losing candidate, Naughton, is eliminated and the second choices on his ballot papers are added up. Of these, O'Neil gets 20, O'Hara 8, Shea 12 and O'Brien 38. The final result of the election is shown on the left.

FINAL RESULT

O'Neil	O'Hara	Shea	O'Brien	Naughton
220	159	112	158	78
ELECTED	ELECTED	LOST	ELECTED	ELIMINATED

Guerrilla warfare

Sometimes a group of people tries to undermine a government* by fighting a **guerrilla war**. This usually consists of acts of violence against the state* carried out by small groups of fighters (**guerrillas**) operating in secret. There are many reasons why guerrillas fight such wars. They may have either revolutionary or nationalistic aims. You can find out more about these below.

People who fight guerrilla wars are not members of a country's permanent armed forces.

Nationalist guerrillas

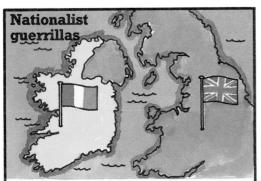

Nationalist guerrillas object to a government* controlled by a different national group to the one they support. For example, guerrilla war plays a part in the IRA campaign* against the British government in Northern Ireland. They are fighting for an Irish government throughout the whole island.

Revolutionary guerrillas

Ordine Nuovo is an Italian counter-revolutionary group who wish to return to Mussolini's* style of government.

Revolutionary guerrillas try to overthrow their country's government* as the first stage in a revolution*. From 1947 to 1949, for example, Mao Zedong (Mao Tse Tung)* waged a guerrilla war against the nationalist* government of China.

   Counter-revolutionary guerrillas seek to return to a former political situation.

Guerrilla tactics

1. War* is not openly declared on the enemy. Instead, secret attacks, called **acts of sabotage**, are made on such things as power stations or army bases. The aim is to destroy them or stop them working in order to weaken the government*.

2. Some guerrillas use **terrorist** tactics to frighten the enemy into giving way. These include random acts of violence against the general public, such as putting bombs in crowded shopping areas.

3. Guerrillas try to get as much publicity as possible in order to focus world attention on their cause and gain supporters. Both sabotage and terrorist methods gain publicity.

Word box

Guerrilla comes from the Spanish word *guerrilla*, meaning little war. This in turn comes from the Spanish word *guerra*, meaning war*.
Ordine Nuovo means "new order" in Italian.
Sabotage comes from the French *saboter*, to make a noise with wooden shoes. (The word *sabot* means a wooden shoe.) In French it also meant to do something badly, or wreck something.
   Someone who carries out acts of sabotage is called a saboteur.
Terrorist comes from the Latin *terror*, meaning fear or terror.

27

*See page 29 for more about revolutions.

Coups d'état and revolutions

Governments° are sometimes changed by force rather than by election°. A country may be invaded by another country. Alternatively, the takeover may come from within the country, by either a coup d'état or a revolution.

A **coup d'état**, or **coup**, is the sudden overthrow of the existing government by a small group, often made up of military officers. The group takes the place of the government and usually works within the existing political system.

In a **revolution**, however, the whole political, social and economic system of a country may be completely changed, involving the support of most of the population.

Coups d'état

Coups usually take place when a government° is in a weak position or there is a **national emergency** such as extreme **civil unrest** (lots of strikes, riots and other evidence of dissatisfaction).

The group carrying out the coup takes control of all means of communication, transport and other services vital to the running of the state°, such as those shown here. The previous government has no means of control left and is prevented from appealing to the people to resist the coup.

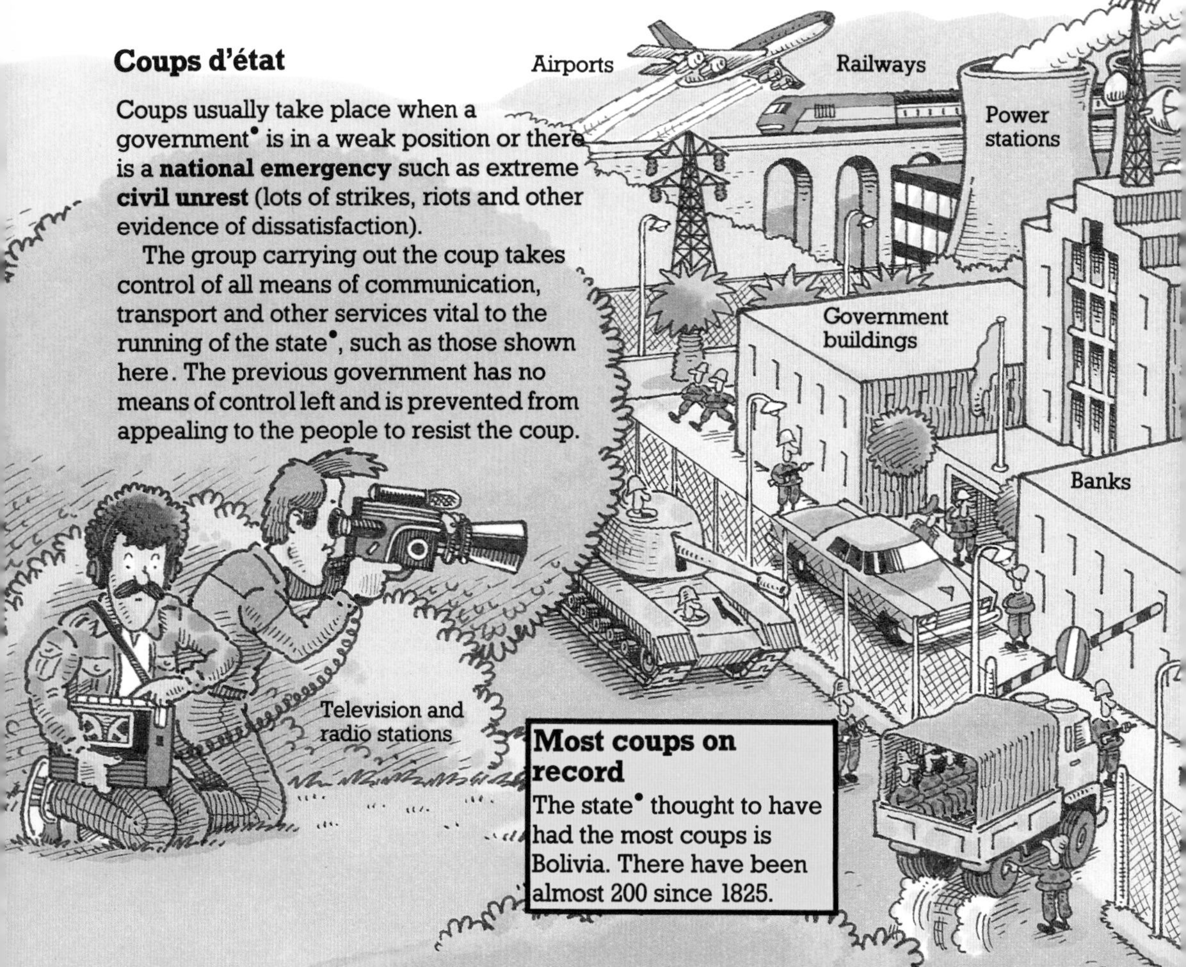

Airports

Railways

Power stations

Government buildings

Banks

Television and radio stations

Most coups on record
The state° thought to have had the most coups is Bolivia. There have been almost 200 since 1825.

A famous coup took place in Chile in 1973. The military under General Augusto Pinochet seized power during a time of instability aggravated by **hyper-inflation**. This means that the value of money goes down rapidly and prices shoot up. Many people suffer because they can afford less and the country can afford fewer **imports** (goods it buys from other countries).

What makes a coup successful?

1. To succeed, coups must be well organized and kept secret.

2. Coups are most likely to succeed where there is support for the existing systems of government° but mistrust of, or lack of confidence in, the leaders.

What happens after a coup?

The picture shows some possible results of a military coup d'état. The bubbles show what might happen at each stage or what the leaders of the coup might be thinking.

Difficult to give up power – country may choose to go back to old government*.

Cut out the opposition – ban political parties and imprison opponents.

Decisions made unconstitutionally* i.e. by a small group, not by representatives* of the people through the legislature*.

Establish group as a new political party. Restore elections and hope to be elected.

Coup d'état

Resolve the country's problems.

Set up military dictatorship.

Control the people – impose curfews*, use the army to help police major cities.

Use force – the army is already trained in such methods.

Hold on to power.

Leaders of a coup often claim that they are taking power only temporarily. They promise to step down once order has been restored or the national emergency is over.

They usually ban political parties* and imprison, without trial, any opponents. They justify this by saying it is part of an attempt to end political conflict and instability. Although they may promise to restore democratic* political rights*, such as elections*, this rarely happens. Many coup leaders are so tempted by political power that they do not want to risk losing it. The coup may result in a military dictatorship*. Coups rarely have the support of the people for long.

Coup or revolution?

Bolsheviks were members of the larger of two groups formed when the Russian Social Democratic Party split in 1903.

Members of the other group were called Mensheviks.

Coups often turn out to be much more than the replacement of one government* by another. Some coups turn into revolutions. For example, the revolution in Russia in 1917 started as a coup d'état with a communist* group called the **Bolsheviks** seizing power from the Tsar*.

Word box

Coup d'état is French for "stroke of the state*" and implies a sudden overthrow of a state's government*.

Revolution comes from the Latin *revolvere*, to turn over. It implies the turning of the wheel of fortune either forward to some ideal state in the future or back to some past ideal.

Hyper-inflation comes from the Greek *hyper*, meaning over, and the Latin *inflatio*, meaning swelling up. The meaning arose through the idea of swelling up like a blown-up balloon.

Import comes from the Latin *importare*, to carry in.

Bolshevik comes from the Russian word *bolshe*, meaning bigger, from *bolshoi*, meaning big.

Menshevik comes from the Russian word, *menshe*, meaning smaller.

A parliamentary system – Britain

The next eight pages describe some different government* systems. Below you can read about the **parliamentary system** of Britain. Britain is sometimes known as the Mother of Parliament as the system developed there. Other countries have borrowed and adapted the parliamentary model.

The beginnings of Parliament

Monarchs* have always needed the support of rich landowners to rule. Anglo-Saxon kings, for example, ruled with the help of the **Witan**. This consisted of 100 leading barons who made laws and raised money and armies for the King. This allowed them to make demands on him in return.

During the 13th century, monarchs found that they needed more money than the barons could supply. They summoned representatives of the people from throughout the country. The two groups formed the basis of the House of Lords (barons) and the House of Commons (ordinary people), later called **Parliament**.

Roundheads

Royalists

There was often conflict between the monarch and Parliament. Civil War broke out in 1642 between the supporters of Charles I (**Royalists**) and the supporters of Parliament (**Roundheads**). The Royalists lost the war and Charles I was beheaded. England became a republic* with Oliver Cromwell as Head of State. When he died, the monarchy was restored. Charles II ruled with a Parliament to help.

How Parliament works
The British Parliament is still headed by the monarch* and divided into the Houses of Lords and Commons. Below you can see how the political system works.

Monarch
Tradition says the monarch* is head of Parliament but monarchs no longer involve themselves directly in government*.

Prime Minister (PM)
The PM is normally the leader of the majority party* in Parliament. He or she is chosen by party members but is still officially appointed by the monarch*.

Role:
★ To appoint and dismiss members of the Cabinet (see below) and other ministers, chosen from party members in Parliament.
★ To lead Cabinet meetings. The PM usually has the last say.
★ To decide the date of a general election*. It must be no later than five years from the last one.

Cabinet
The **Cabinet** is a committee of senior government* ministers chosen by the Prime Minister. These ministers head the major departments of state. These include the Treasury, the Departments of Education and the Environment and the Ministry of Defence.

Role:
★ To make major policy* decisions.
★ To decide which proposed laws (known as **Bills**) will go before Parliament for debate and when.
★ To co-ordinate the work of government* departments and settle policy differences between them.

Other ministers
More junior ministers help senior ministers and head less important departments. People working under them are known as **Civil Servants**. They are permanent administrative staff. They advise on and carry out government* policy*.

Shadow ministers

The second largest party in Parliament (the **Opposition**) appoints its own spokespeople, known as **shadow ministers**. They criticize government ministers' decisions and suggest alternatives to government policy[•].

House of Lords

This consists of **hereditary peers** (people with inherited titles), **life peers** (those who have been rewarded by the monarch[•] with titles which cannot be inherited), **law lords** (top judges) and Church of England **archbishops** and **bishops**.

Role:
★ They can propose their own Bills.
★ They vote on Bills passed by the House of Commons. If they oppose a Bill it goes back to the Commons. If the Commons pass it again, the Bill becomes law in one year's time despite the Lords' opposition.

House of Commons

This is made up of 650 elected[•] constituency[•] representatives[•] or **Members of Parliament (MPs)**.

Role:
★ MPs debate and vote[•] on Bills proposed by both Houses. The party[•] in government[•] normally has a majority in the House of Commons, so it can usually get support for its Bills.
★ MPs examine government policy[•].
★ MPs represent their constituents'[•] interests. Most hold meetings, called **surgeries**, in their constituencies[•] to discuss people's problems.
★ MPs occasionally introduce their own Bills, called **Private Members' Bills**.

Electorate

The **electorate** consists of British people who are eligible to vote.* They elect MPs into the House of Commons.

The Palace of Westminster

The Houses of Commons and Lords are known as the **Houses of Parliament**. They meet in the **Palace of Westminster**, shown below.

The Prime Minister and government ministers form the executive[•]. The monarch[•] and the Houses of Parliament form the legislature[•]. The roles of the executive and the legislature are not entirely separate. The executive depends on the support of the House of Commons to remain in office and Cabinet members belong to both the executive and the legislature.

Word box
Parliament comes from the Medieval Latin *parliamentum*, based on the Late Latin word *parabolare*, to talk.
Witan comes from the Old English *wita*, meaning wise man.
Cabinet comes from the word cabin, meaning a small room. It refers to the private room where the council of ministers meets with the Prime Minister.
Peer (an Anglo-Norman word) comes from the Latin *par*, meaning equal in rank.

*See page 23 for more about voting and elections.

A presidential system – the USA

Unlike the British system of government° which developed through the centuries, the American system was carefully thought out in the 18th century.

In 1775, people living in Britain's American colonies° rebelled against paying taxes to Britain. This was the **War of Independence**. The British were defeated in 1781. In 1783 the two countries signed a contract, called a **treaty**, recognizing the United States of America as an independent nation.

The American Constitution

After gaining independence°, Americans had to decide how their country should be governed. They wrote a constitution* which was not completed until 1787. They created three branches of government°: the President (the executive°), Congress (the legislature°) and the Supreme Court (the judiciary°). One of the main aims was to prevent any one branch of government from having too much power.

The President

A **President** is elected° for a four year **term**, or period, and can serve a maximum of two four-year terms.

Role:

★ The President is head of the Executive Office which carries out government° policy°.

★ The President can introduce Bills° through a supporter in Congress. He is responsible for introducing the Bill concerning the annual **budget**.

★ The President can **veto** (reject) Bills passed by Congress. However, a Bill can still become law if two-thirds of both Houses of Congress° vote° in its favour.

★ The President manages foreign affairs and can make treaties subject to a two-thirds majority vote in the Senate.

★ He is Commander of the Armed Forces and can send troops abroad or use them to keep order at home.

The Cabinet

The **Cabinet** is chosen by the President, but traditionally includes the heads of the major departments and sometimes the **Vice** (deputy) **President**.

"Noes 7, Ayes 1; the Ayes have it."

A "No" vote is against the proposal. An "Aye" vote is for it.

The Cabinet advises the President, though he may ignore its advice. Above you can see what President Lincoln once said when he disagreed with the result of a Cabinet vote°.

The President lives and works in the **White House** in Washington D.C.

White House staff

The White House staff consists of the President's advisors and assistants. They prepare information to give to the press, for instance.

*See pages 18-19 for more about constitutions.

Congress

Congress is made up of two Houses, the **Senate** (the **Upper House**) and the **House of Representatives** (the **Lower House**).

The Senate
Each state*elects* two representatives* called **Senators** to the **Senate**. Senators are elected for six years but they do not all get elected at the same time. One third of the total number is elected every second year to give continuity.

The House of Representatives
This consists of 435 Representatives* who serve for two years. The number elected* by each state* is determined by the state's population.

Role of Congress
★ Members from both Houses introduce and vote* on new Bills*.
★ Congress can make **amendments** (changes) to the President's proposals.
★ Each House checks any Bills passed by the other House.
★ The President must get Senate approval before appointing certain senior staff such as the Secretaries (Ministers) heading the major departments.

Supreme Court
The **Supreme Court** consists of judges chosen by the President and approved by the Senate.

Role:
★ They can declare a law unconstitutional*.
★ The Court interprets the law, deciding what any controversial law means.

Presidents and Parliaments

A presidential system is distinct from a parliamentary* system in these ways:

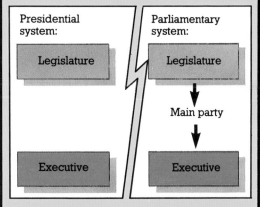

1. In a presidential system, the executive* and legislature* are separate. No one can hold office in both branches. This is known as **separation of powers**. Each branch serves as a check on the actions of the other.

In a parliamentary system, the executive (Prime Minister* and ministers) is made up of members of the legislature and is normally formed from the majority party* in the legislature.

2. In a presidential system, the general public elect* the executive in the form of a President.

In a parliamentary system, the main party or parties in the legislature elect the leader of the executive.

A country with a President does not necessarily have a presidential system. In some parliamentary systems, a President is elected as well as a Prime Minister, but has only ceremonial duties similar to that of a monarch*.

National and state powers
America has a federal system of government (see pages 18-19). States* can make their own laws on subjects such as marriage and divorce, fire precautions, police and education.

The President and Congress alone can make laws on such things as declaring war, producing money and creating new national courts.

A one-party system – the USSR

The USSR is a one-party state[•] dominated by the **Communist Party of the Soviet Union** (the **CPSU** or **Party**). There is a federal[•] system of government[•] but individual states[•] have fewer powers than, say, the states in the USA. Russia claims to be still in the transitional socialist stage[•] first described by Marx[•] and adapted by Lenin[•]. Full communism[•], where there is no need for a central governing body, has not come about.

The move towards communism

Before 1917, Russia was an autocracy[•] dominated by rulers called Tsars[•]. In 1917, revolution[•] broke out. The Tsar abdicated[•] and Russia was proclaimed a republic[•]. There was then a struggle for power between various revolutionary groups. It was won by the Bolshevik[•] party[•], led by Lenin*. The Bolsheviks wanted power to be in the hands of councils of workers, called **Soviets**.

In 1918, the republic was named the Russian Soviet Federal Socialist Republic (RSFSR). The Union of Soviet Socialist Republics (USSR) was formed in 1922 when more socialist[•] republics such as the Ukraine and Belorussia joined the RSFSR.

The seat of government[•] is the **Kremlin** in Moscow.

Who are the members of the CPSU?

The CPSU consists of people who are interested in politics[•] and active in promoting the Party. About 9% of the population are admitted for membership. They must have certain qualifications and must be dedicated to the CPSU.

The CPSU is headed by a committee of about 12 members called the **Politburo**. In the past they controlled the USSR by making all the important decisions and appointing top people. Under Gorbachev their powers have been reduced. The Politburo is headed by a **General Secretary**. Although he has generally held office for life or until unseated by a coup, this is likely to change as the new political system evolves.

The executive and legislature

The executive[•] consists of a **Council of Ministers**. Members head departments of state[•] and carry out government[•] policy[•].

Gorbachev reorganised the legislature[•] to make it more democratic[•]. It consists of two bodies, the **Congress of People's Deputies** (elected[•] by the people), and the **Supreme Soviet** (elected by the Congress).

The Supreme Soviet has two chambers, which work in a similar way to Western parliaments[•]. Before, it was just a rubber stamp for decisions made by the CPSU.

As a result of constitutional[•] changes introduced in 1990, the most important position in the Supreme Soviet is the **Prezident**. The Prezident has far greater powers than those of Western leaders.

*You can find out more about Lenin on page 11.

The role of the CPSU

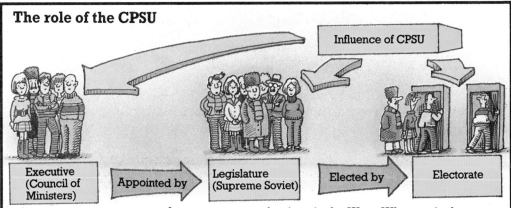

Influence of CPSU

Executive (Council of Ministers)	Appointed by	Legislature (Supreme Soviet)	Elected by	Electorate

After the Russian revolution*, the CPSU became the only officially recognised political party* in the USSR. But as a result of recent changes, it has been deprived of its monopoly, and new parties have emerged to challenge it. Also, many of its powers have been transferred to the Supreme Soviet and other political institutions.

Elections too are much more like elections in the West. Whereas in the past, communist candidates were returned automatically, now they have to compete for votes*. In elections in 1989 and 1990, many party officials were defeated.

In some Soviet republics, such as Lithuania, national parties are becoming stronger than the CPSU. Several of these parties want to break from the USSR and establish independent states*.

> The aim of the Pioneers is to teach children discipline and a love of learning and also to help them to understand the communist ideology and the Russian system.

Education and the CPSU

The CPSU teaches the communist* ideology* to children through two **Youth Leagues**: the **Pioneers** for 9-11 year olds and **Komsomol**, for 11-18 year olds. Both are closely involved in children's schooling.

The media

The Russian newspaper Pravda.

In the past, the CPSU controlled Russian television, radio and press (the media). Nowadays the media is much freer and can publish things that were previously forbidden.

The spoken word

The constitution* states that no one may "injure the interests of society and state" by criticizing them. However, although people are not supposed to criticize what the CPSU stands for, they are encouraged to discuss and suggest better ways for it to put communist* theory into practice.

The KGB

This is the security police force. It has been the muscle behind the Communist regime since 1917. It is still the backbone of the Soviet system, despite Gorbachev's reforms.

Word box

Soviet is the Russian word for a council of delegates or representatives*.
Praesidium comes from the Latin *praesidere,* meaning to preside over or direct. This is based on the Latin *prae* (before) and *sedere* (sit).
Politburo comes from the Russian *politbyuro.* This word is based on *politicheskii,* meaning political, and *byuro,* meaning bureau or office.
Pravda means truth in Russian.

The largest democracy – India

India is the largest democracy* in the world, with about 600,000,000 people and about 250,000,000 voters*. The system of government* is a mixture of the British parliamentary* system and the American presidential* system. Like America, it is a federal* system with both central and state* governments.

Over the last two centuries, India has changed from being a collection of monarchies*, to being under British colonial* rule, to being an independent state*.

The story of India

In the 18th century, India consisted of many separate kingdoms. There were many different religions amongst the kingdoms, such as Islam, Hinduism and Buddhism.

Mahatma Gandhi (1869-1948)

The British East India Company, which was a very large trading company, started to establish colonial* rule in India at about this time to further its business. The Company was brought under British government* control in 1784 because of wars* between the Company, the French (who also had trade interests) and the native princes. The first British Governor-General of India was appointed in 1784. He was responsible to the British government for the way India was run.

British colonial rule continued until 1947 when India was granted independence*. This was largely due to a popular campaign* led by **Mahatma Gandhi**. He encouraged non-violent methods such as strikes and mass rallies to show the Indian people's resistance to British colonial rule. This is known as **passive resistance**. He was **assassinated** (murdered) by a member of an anti-Gandhi organization as he walked to a prayer meeting.

India became a democratic* republic* and the Indian constitution* came into being in January 1950.

The Indian government

India's constitution* is the longest written constitution in the world. Below you can find out about the structure of the central government*.

The executive*
This consists of the President, the Prime Minister and the Council of Ministers.

President
Unlike in the USA, the President has very little political power in practice. Any decision he or she comes to is made on the advice and with the approval of the Council of Ministers who are responsible to the legislature* (see below). The President is elected* by the central and state legislatures.

Prime Minister
As in Britain, the Prime Minister is the leader of the largest party* in the legislature.

Council of Ministers
The Council of Ministers is made up of all the ministers and deputies of the major departments. They are appointed by the President on the advice of the Prime Minister.

The Council of Ministers rarely meets. A select group of senior ministers is the major policy-making body in the Indian political system. This is called the Cabinet*.

As in the UK, the Prime Minister and Cabinet rely on party members in the legislature to pass proposals.

Parliament House

Legislature

The legislature° consists of two Houses of Parliament, the **Lok Sabha** and the **Rajya Sabha**. They sit in a building called Parliament House, shown in the picture above. Parliament House is situated in New Delhi. Below you can find out more about the Lok Sabha and the Rajya Sabha.

1. Lok Sabha (House of the People)

Indian citizens° elect° about 500 members to this House every five years.

2. Rajya Sabha (Council of States)

There are about 250 members of the Rajya Sabha. Most of these are representatives° of Indian states°, chosen by their state's legislature. However, 12 are appointed directly by the President and have a special knowledge of either the arts, literature, science or social services.

As in the USA, all executive° proposals must be approved by both the Lok Sabha and the Rajya Sabya.

Political problems

1. There are 15 different major languages spoken in India's 21 states. This can make it difficult, for example, to spread information about a political party°.

2. There are six major religious groups: Hindus, Moslems, Christians, Sikhs, Buddhists and Jains. Differences between religious groups have lead to demands for political independence and the break-up of the state°.

Over 15,200,000 ballot boxes° are needed for an Indian general election.

3. Being the largest democracy° in the world, elections° have to be very efficiently organized.

Multistate political parties

If a political party° tries to win seats° in more than one state° and gets more than 4% of the votes°, it is known as a **multistate party**. A multistate party can have its own party symbol. This is very important because many citizens° in India cannot read or write. Voters often look for the symbol rather than the name of the party or the name of the candidate°.

Word box

Resistance comes from the Latin word *resistere,* to withstand or resist.

Assassinate comes from the Arabic word *hassassin* hashish-men, the name of a Shiite sect which murdered their enemies' leaders. It flourished between the 11th and 13th centuries. Its victims included some of the Crusaders. The killers intoxicated themselves with hashish before carrying out orders.

37

Diplomacy and spying

For thousands of years, people have been exploring and trading with other countries. This often led to arguments and war[*]. Countries began to negotiate and make agreements with each other in an attempt to keep the peace and promote trade. This is known as **diplomacy**.

The story of diplomacy

1. In very early societies, a person would be appointed to travel to another group in order to obtain information and deliver important messages. This person was called an **emissary**.

Emissary

2. In the 15th century, Italian states[*] sent representatives to live in the capital cities of other states. Their task was originally to promote trade between the states. They were called **diplomats**.

3. The diplomats' role soon grew. For instance, they helped to keep the peace by sorting out disagreements before they led to war[*]. By the 18th century many other states in Europe had diplomats.

4. Today, most states have diplomats based in many other countries. This is despite the fact that political ideologies[*] and systems vary a great deal between different countries.

Diplomatic rules

For diplomacy to work, countries must be sure that their diplomats will not be harmed in any way and that communications between a diplomat and the home government[*] will remain confidential. For this reason, there are various international laws to protect diplomats and their premises, or **embassies**. This is known as **diplomatic immunity**.

The **diplomatic bag**, or **black bag**, is used to carry messages from a diplomat to his or her government. It must not be tampered with and can go through Customs unsearched.

What do diplomats do?

1. They represent their country's government[*] abroad. This shows the goodwill of their country. Alternatively, if a country wishes to show its disapproval of another, it can recall some of its diplomats.

2. They obtain information about the state[*], such as its foreign policies[*] and military strength. This is known as **intelligence**. They also assess the effect this information will have on their own country.

3. They protect their country's citizens[*] overseas. This includes everything from helping a tourist who has lost a passport to getting citizens out of prison or out of a country that is at war[*].

A country's chief diplomat in another country is called an **ambassador**. He or she lives and works in an embassy.

Obtaining information openly

Most of a diplomat's information is obtained in ways approved by the foreign government*. These include reading newspapers and magazines, watching television and listening to the radio.

Diplomats also attend dinners and parties where they meet important politicians, business people, trade union* leaders and so on. They talk to them and try to pick up useful information.

Spying

Most countries also try to find out secret information. This is called **spying**, or **espionage**. If the people doing this, called **spies**, are caught, they are sent home.

Spies make contact with people willing to sell information such as military secrets. They also secretly meet people who are opposed to the political system. These are **dissidents**. All this can help a spy assess a country's true strengths and weaknesses.

A famous spy
A famous spy was Kim Philby who worked for the Soviet Union although he was British. He was employed at the centre of the British Secret Intelligence Service in the 1940s and early 1950s. During that time he was actually spying for the Russians. This allowed him to send some of Britain's most important secrets straight to Moscow.

CONFIDENTIAL

Word box

Diplomacy and **diplomat** are both based on the Greek word *diploma*, meaning a folded paper, or letter of recommendation.
Emissary comes from the Latin word *emissarius*, scout or spy. This is based on *emittere*, to send out.
Ambassador and **embassy** are both based on the Latin word *ambactus*, a vassal or servant. This is because an ambassador is a servant of his or her country.
Intelligence is from the Latin word *intelligentia*, understanding or intelligence.
Spy is a short form of espy, meaning to catch sight of or observe. It is from the Old French word *espier*. **Espionage** is from the later French word *espion*, a spy.
Dissident comes from the Latin word *dissidere*, to disagree. It literally means to sit apart (*dis-* means apart, and *sedere* means to sit).

Spying by satellite
Another useful way of obtaining information about another country is by satellite. Satellites can take detailed pictures from miles up in the sky. They can collect information such as the movement of a country's troops and the state of its industry and agriculture. Special satellites, called "Early warning satellites", can detect the launch of a nuclear missile.

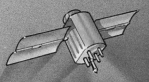

39

Persuasion and disagreement

Most disagreements between countries are dealt with by government⁰ leaders and diplomats⁰ from one state⁰ talking to those of the other. However, there are other methods of persuasion. Some are used as back-ups or alternatives to diplomacy⁰. Others are used as a last resort when diplomacy fails. You can find out about these methods below.

1. Propaganda

Propaganda⁰ is information intended to win support. A country may use propaganda to sway world opinion in its favour or against other countries. By communicating directly with people in another country, it aims to persuade them to put pressure on their government⁰ to change its policies⁰.

Governments often transmit propaganda on short-wave radio which can be heard over great distances. Both Russia and America have radio stations for this, called Radio Moscow and the Voice of America. Each has over 100 programmes broadcast in various languages, through which it puts its view of world events.

Radios are cheap and even the illiterate in poor states can follow broadcasts.

Propaganda can help a group in another country. For instance, after the 1986 elections⁰ in the Philippines, the Voice of America publicized the belief that it had been rigged⁰ by the former President Marcos. This helped the case of the other candidate⁰, Cory Aquino, who became the President⁰.

2. Economic pressure

When a state⁰ puts **economic pressure** on another, it threatens to damage it financially. The poorer the state, the more effective the economic pressure is likely to be. Below you can see the two main kinds of economic pressure.

a. Granting and withholding aid

Often rich countries give or lend money to poorer countries who support their policies⁰. They may refuse to give aid to governments⁰ they disapprove of. Threats to withhold aid can be used to encourage governments to change their policies.

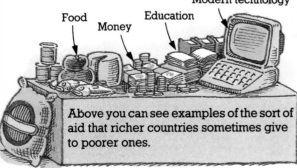

Modern technology

Food

Money

Education

Above you can see examples of the sort of aid that richer countries sometimes give to poorer ones.

b. Trade sanctions

A **trade sanction** is applied when one state stops part or all of its trade with another to apply pressure or express anger. For example, when Russia invaded Afghanistan in 1979, the USA banned the sale of American grain to Russia.

Some governments, including many African states, have imposed trade sanctions on South Africa by refusing to trade with the country. This shows their disapproval of the apartheid⁰ system in South Africa.

Another way of imposing sanctions on a country is to refuse to play sports against them.

Many people believe that sanctions against South Africa should be extended to all kinds of sporting and social contacts. This is known as **boycotting** South Africa.

3. Military pressure and war

If other methods fail, force or the threat of force may be used. This can be done in the following ways:

Deterrence is an attempt by a state• to deter or dissuade other states from attacking it by building up its armed forces. In practice, this usually leads to an **arms race**, where each state tries to stay one step ahead in terms of the number and the power of its weapons.

Subversion is an attempt by a state to overthrow another government• by giving support to rebels fighting that government. Rivalry between the USSR and the USA in the post-war period has produced many examples of subversion being used by each side to gain influence, especially in the Third World.

Threats of force may be made by a government to show that it is prepared to use military action if the state offending it does not give way. For example, in the early 1980s, the USSR threatened to invade Poland if its government did not restrict the free trade union movement (Solidarity).

Reprisal raids are armed attacks made to punish a state for acting against the first state's interests. The USA resorted to a reprisal bombing raid on Libya, after earlier threats of force failed.

War is used mainly as a last resort, for example, when one country feels threatened by events in another, or to extend its power and acquire wealth. Sometimes war occurs when events get out of control. The First World War started with the assassination of an Austrian Archduke which set off a chain reaction, producing a conflict that eventually involved all major world powers. In contrast, the Second World War was provoked by Hitler's aggressive designs on neighbouring states.

Word box

Economic is from the Greek word *oikonomia* which means household management. It is based on the words *oikos* (a house) and *nemein* (to manage or administer).

Sanction comes from the Latin word *sanctio* which means a binding decree.

Boycott came from Captain C.C. Boycott (1832-1897) who was in charge of the estate of the Earl of Erne in County Mayo. The tenants (people who rented the houses and land on the estate) refused to have anything to do with him.

Deterrence comes from the Latin *deterrere* meaning to frighten off, or deter.

Subversion is from the Latin *subversio*, meaning I overthrow. It is based on the Latin words *sub*, meaning under or from under, and *vertere*, to turn.

Rebel is from the Latin word *rebellis*, which means making war again. The Latin word *bellum* means war.

Reprisal comes from the Latin word *reprehendere*, which means to seize again or to seize by way of retaliation.

War comes from Anglo-Norman *werre*, which was taken from a Germanic word *werra*, meaning strife.

International organizations and alliances

At various times, countries have entered into formal relationships with each other for their military, commercial or cultural benefit. On these pages you can find out about some of the major alliances and international organizations that exist today and what their main aims and functions are.

United Nations (UN)

Formed: 1945

Members today: About 160 member states.

Aims: International peace and security.

What it does: The UN tries to find solutions to international problems through its various organs. These include the General Assembly, where every state has one vote, and the Security Council which mediates in conflicts which threaten to turn into war. The Security Council has fifteen members, of which five – USA, USSR, UK, France and China – are permanent. These five also possess a veto. The UN has a permanent Secretariat headed by the Secretary-General. There is also an Economic and Social Council, which deals with health, education and human rights, for example.

It has also set up various agencies to deal with specific problems, such as UNESCO (United Nations Educational, Scientific and Cultural Organization), UNICEF (United Nations International Children's Emergency Fund) and WHO (World Health Organization).

UN Peacekeeping forces, made up of mixed troops from the member countries, have sometimes been used. In the early 1950s, UN forces expelled invading communist North Korean forces from South Korea, while at other times they have provided peace-keeping forces.

The International Court of Justice has 15 judges.

The UN provides a neutral place where diplomatic relations between countries locked in conflict can be maintained.

Problems: It is hard to resolve issues as all permanent members of the Security Council must agree to actions.

A country may exploit the UN for propaganda purposes. It may claim to want UN approval but have no intention of acting on its proposals.

North Atlantic Treaty Organization (NATO)

Formed: 1949

Members today: Belgium, France, Luxembourg, UK, Netherlands, Canada, Denmark, Iceland, Italy, Norway, USA, Spain, Portugal, Greece, Turkey, West Germany.

Aims: To create a military alliance against the power of the USSR. Founded at the time when suspicion between East and West was at its height (the Cold War).

What it does: The NATO countries cooperate in a security policy for the Western world by maintaining strong defence forces. The Military Committee deals with military matters. It consists of members from every NATO country except France, which opted out in 1966, and Iceland, which has no armed forces.

Other NATO committees cover non-military matters, such as finance or politics.

Problems: The reduction of the Soviet threat and disintegration of the Warsaw Pact poses the question of why NATO is still needed. NATO is responding to this by de-emphasising its military character and taking on a more political role.

Warsaw Pact

Founded: 1955

Members today: Russia, Bulgaria, East Germany, Hungary, Poland, Romania, Czechoslovakia.

Aims: Formation of an alliance of European countries to oppose NATO. Agreement to support each other against outside aggression.

What it does: Ministers of Defence and military leaders of member countries meet on the Political Consultative Committee.

Problems: The fall of communist regimes in Eastern Europe and the reunification of Germany deprives it of its members and structure. Unless it works with the West for common security, it will wither away.

European Communities

Founded: Negotiations between founder members (Belgium, France, West Germany, Italy, Luxembourg and the Netherlands) started in 1950. In 1951, the Treaty of Paris was signed, creating the European Coal and Steel Community (ECSC). The European Economic Community (EEC) and the European Atomic Energy Community (EAEC or Euratom) were created in 1957 when the founder members signed the Treaties of Rome.

Members today: Belgium, France, West Germany, Italy, Netherlands, Luxembourg, Denmark, UK, Ireland, Greece, Spain, Portugal.

Aims: To promote European union, eventually making Europe one state and thus preventing nationalism* causing another European war.

What they do: The executive body of the Communities is the European Commission, which works independently of any single country for the benefit of the whole Community.

In addition, there is the Council of Ministers which consists of ministers from each country looking after their national interests. The Council shares decision-making powers with the European Parliament on a wide range of issues. The European Parliament consists of elected representatives from each country, and its powers are increasing.

Another particularly important institution is the European Court of Justice which is the supreme court* of the European Community.

The European Economic Community has introduced many schemes such as the Common Agricultural Policy and the European Monetary System.

Problems: Patriotism and nationalism still stand in the way of agreement much of the time (see pages 6-7 for more about this).

Organization of African Unity (OAU)

Founded: 1963

Members today: 32 African countries.

Aims: To eliminate colonialism in Africa, to further African unity and to co-ordinate policies for development.

What it does: Member countries attempt to co-ordinate political, economic, cultural, scientific and defence policies. They oppose apartheid and have refused to let South Africa join the OAU.

The Commonwealth of Nations

Founded (in its modern form): 1949

Members today: 49 countries (all former members of the British Empire)

Aims: Mutual co-operation and assistance.

What it does: These countries maintain formal and informal diplomatic contacts, assisted by the Commonwealth Secretariat.

The Arab League

Founded: 1945

Founders: Iraq, Syria, Saudi Arabia, Lebanon, Jordan, Yemen, Egypt.

Members today: 21 Arab states (Egypt's membership suspended 1979).

Aims: To unite the various Arab states. Today, the League opposes the continued existence of the State of Israel.

What it does: The Arab League represents the interests of the Arab world internationally.

It has abolished customs duties on agricultural products and natural resources exported within the League.

Political parties of the world

The charts on these pages show the main political parties in many countries, and what they stand for. They also tell you the titles of their political leaders and the names of their political institutions.

COUNTRY	MAIN POLITICAL PARTIES	POLITICAL INSTITUTIONS	POLITICAL LEADERS
Australia	**Labour** – socialist democratic **Liberal** – liberal/conservative **National (Country)** – for free enterprise	Senate House of Representatives	Governor General Prime Minister
Canada	**Liberal** – centre* **Progressive Conservative** – for free enterprise; pro-NATO **New Democratic** – social-democratic	Senate House of Commons	Governor General Prime Minister
China	**Communist Party** – for the socialist modernization of China	National People's Congress	State President Chairman of the Communist Party
France	**Socialist** – democratic-socialist **Communist** **"Gaullist" (Association for the Republic)** – conservative; nationalist **Union of French Democracy** – liberal/conservative **National Front** – extreme right	National Assembly Senate	President of the Republic Prime Minister
Republic of Ireland	**Fine Gail** – centre/right **Fianna Fail** – centre/left **Labour** – democratic–socialist **Sinn Fein** – supports the IRA•	Dail Eireann (Parliament)	President of the Republic Taoiseach (Prime Minister)
Federal Republic of Germany	**Social Democratic** – centre*/left **Christian Democratic** – centre/right; conservative **Free Democratic** – centre **Christian Socialist** – right **Greens** – for conservation; anti nuclear power	Bundestag (Lower House) Bundesrat (Upper House)	Federal President Federal Chancellor
India	**Indian National Congress** – socialist (democratic) **Janata** – centre*/right **Communist Party of India**	Council of States (Rajya Sabha) House of the People (Lok Sabha)	President of the Republic Prime Minister

44

*Centre is between left-wing and right-wing.

COUNTRY	MAIN POLITICAL PARTIES	POLITICAL INSTITUTIONS	POLITICAL LEADERS
Israel	**Labour Party** – socialist (democratic) **Likud** – right-wing nationalist **National Religious Party** – to apply Jewish law to daily life	Knesset	President Prime Minister
Italy	**Christian Democratic** – Roman Catholic (left, centre and right) **Communist** – independent communist, 'Eurocommunist' **Italian Social Movement** – extreme right **Socialist** – left **Social Democratic** – centre; socialist	Senate Chamber of Deputies	President of the Republic Prime Minister
New Zealand	**Labour** – socialist **National** – centre **Social Credit** – for monetary reform policy	House of Representatives	Governor General Prime Minister
Russia (USSR)	**Communist Party** – socialist; state-ownership of property	Supreme Soviet	Chairman of the Praesidium of the Supreme Soviet/President General Secretary of the CPSU Chairman of the Council of Ministers
Spain	**Spanish Workers' Socialist Party** – militant left **Alliance** – extreme right **Centre Democratic Union** – centre/moderate right **Basque Nationalist** – for autonomy of Basque region **Communist** **Social and Democratic Centre** – centre party with strong church support	Cortes (made up of Senate and Congress of Deputies)	Monarch President/Prime Minister
Great Britain	**Labour** – left; socialist (democratic) **Conservative** – right **Liberal Democrat** – centre **Social Democrat** – centre	House of Commons House of Lords	Monarch Prime Minister
United States of America	**Republican** – emphasis on restraining central government and maintaining state rights **Democratic** – more emphasis on Federal programmes	Senate House of Representatives	President

Index

In this index, you will see that some page numbers are in bold. A bold number tells you that the word is defined on that page.

47